Homemade Repellents:
10 Organic Non-Toxic Mosquito and Ant Repellents

Table of content

Introduction

In this book, you will be learning how you could make your own homemade ants and mosquito repellents. I have given 5 recipes of how you can make mosquito repellents for you and your family. I have given another 5 recipes of how you can make ant killers and repellents.

If you understand why natural repellents are better than synthetic repellents or killers, you would quickly switch to natural products. You can make these natural recipes at your home with your own hands.

To keep a home clean, it is very important that you don't have ants always lurking around your house. For this, it is very important that you take care of the ant problem which is at its peak during the spring season. The 5 recipes that I have given in this book are really easy and useful to not only keep yourself safe from ant attacks but also kill them when needed. Ants make huge colonies in spring season at different points in your house and it is very difficult to deal with such a huge amount of ants. I have solved this problem for you by giving you recipes in one chapter on how you could destroy the whole colonies once and for all. The best part is that you can find all the ingredients required to make the repellents or killers, in your kitchen.

Mosquito repellents are very important to keep your family safe from mosquito bites. Mosquito bites can cause many serious fevers so you have to keep yourself safe from mosquitoes. You can use the synthetic products available in the market but they will only work well for you in the beginning. You will realize that, in the long run, they are causing serious damages to your health and skin. For this, it is suggested that you use homemade natural mosquito repellents. You can make these with simple ingredients from your kitchen. I have shared 5 really useful recipes of making mosquito repellents.

Chapter 1 – How to Keep Mosquitoes and Ants Out of Your House

Everyone faces these problems in his/her life when he/she has to face lots of ants and mosquitoes taking residence in his/her house. Their presence is not only annoying; it also shows the lack of hygiene in your household. To keep these things away from your house, you have to take certain measures. The first thing is to keep your house neat and clean. Don't leave food chunks on the floor or on your kitchen shelves. Ants attack especially in the spring season. Mosquitoes also breed in dirty places. So first, you have to make sure your household is not welcoming to ants and mosquitoes. Now, how can you get rid of these things? Let's have a look how you can take care of these problems one by one,

Ants:

http://pestworldforkids.org/media/12886/Small-Ants.jpg

You can kill the ants by the following ways,

- Take a cucumber and cut it into small slices. Place these slices at different entrance corners of your kitchen. Ants avoid the scent of cucumber. If you use a bitter cucumber, it would be much better.

- Spray soap water to kill ants and to keep them from moving into your house.

- Crush mint leaves or mint tea leaves and use them to kill or repel ants.

- Make a mixture of mint apply jelly with boric acid to kill pharaoh ants.

- Pour soap solution in the cracks where ants have taken residence. You can also put cut out cloves in the crack to kill ants.

- You can also destroy the whole colonies by this simple method. Take a liter of water, borax (1 tsp) and a cup of sugar. Now take some cotton balls and dip them in the solution. Take a yogurt container and make holes in it to allow the ants inside the container. Put these cotton balls in the container. The ants would carry these baits to their colonies and the whole colony would die with the smell of the bait or upon eating it.

Mosquitoes:

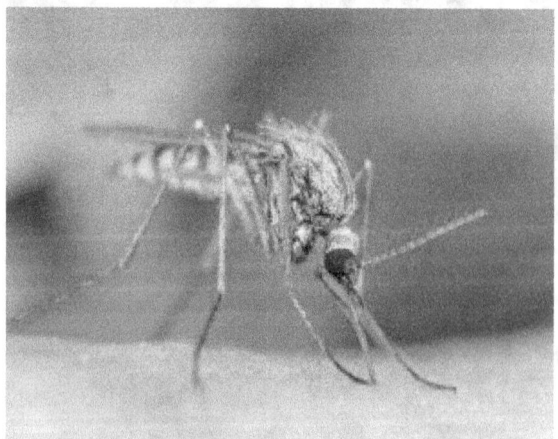

Kill the mosquitoes by the following ways,

- Mosquitoes breed and stay in areas where water is standing or in places that are dirty. So the first thing you should do to keep yourself safe from mosquitoes is to keep your house clean and don't let water standing anywhere and keep the containers containing water covered.

- Make a solution of garlic juice and spray this on your body to keep mosquitoes away from you. The smell of garlic would repel the mosquitoes for the next 6 hours. Make this spray by mixing one part of garlic juice and five parts of water. Put this in a spray bottle and use it on your body. This is non-toxic and really effective.

- You can use natural neem oil that is extracted from neem leaves. This is also very effective in keeping the mosquitoes away from you. This solution is non-toxic. You can apply neem oil on your skin to keep it safe from mosquito bites. Neem oil is also very good for your skin to keep harmful bacteria from attacking your immune system.

- You can use the marigold plant to keep bugs and mosquitoes away from your home. The fragrance of this plant keeps bugs and mosquitoes away. Plant marigold in your garden or yard to keep the mosquitoes away.

- Thai lemon grass is another plant that is very good at keeping mosquitoes away. Take a stalk of this plant and peel off the leaves from the stalk. Now peel off the layers from the stalk until you find a scallion like stem. Use this stem and rub it in your palm strongly. The stem would turn to pulp and you would get a juicy mass in your palm. You can rub this juice over your body and mosquitoes would stay away from you.

If you follow these instructions, you would be able to get rid of mosquitoes and ants in no time.

Chapter 2 – Benefits of Using Natural & Homemade Products

Why should you use natural and homemade products to protect yourself from mosquitoes and ants when you can buy them from the market? If you use different chemical and artificial products to keep ants and mosquitoes away, you would feel satisfied with them but that is because you don't know about the benefits of natural and homemade products. We feel satisfied with our present routines and don't want to switch to something else until we realize that something better is out there and that it is a much better replacement for what we are using at the present.

http://atando-cabos.com/images/mosquito.jpg

To know how something is better than what we are using right now, you just have to compare the benefits of both. After a fair comparison, you can judge for yourself which is better for you and if you should replace your present product with something even better.

In this chapter, I would like to share with you some benefits of natural and homemade products that you cannot get from using artificial or chemical products. After knowing the benefits, I would leave it to you to judge what you want to use in the future. Let's have a look at the benefits of homemade and natural products:

1. **Homemade and natural products are earth-friendly.**

Products that are made conventionally have a very bad effect on our environment. Our environment is already facing many dangerous situations that are to be dealt with seriously. When these chemical and artificial products are manufactured, they cause a lot of air pollution. The air gets polluted by the harmful chemicals used and exhausted in the manufacturing of these products. These industries damage the water too when they throw the chemical wastes in the rivers, canals and lakes etc. A huge amount of these chemicals also goes down your drain in your home daily. Natural products are not harmful at all. They are made organically and in a safe environment. They don't require chemical reactions and additions to be produced. They are mostly made manually and no harmful chemicals are released into the air or water. The land on which they are made is also safe. The environmentalists put a lot of emphasis on using products that are organic and natural and that are made at home so that the environment can be safe from the harmful effects of the chemical and artificial products.

2. Natural and homemade products don't cause irritation.

Products that are made on a commercial and industrial level require the use of chemicals, artificial colors, odors and fillers. These things are harmful to the skin and they can cause redness on your skin. These artificial products, on making contact with skin, especially the sensitive type, they may cause irritation or even breakout. People with sensitive skins often get irritation and itchiness after the use of chemical and artificial products. Products that are made at home are very friendly to your skin because they are closer to nature and they work with your skin instead of working against it providing protection to all kinds of skins and especially the sensitive ones.

3. Natural and homemade products are anti-allergic.

Products that are made at home do not cause allergic reactions on your skin. People who have allergies are advised to use products that are made from natural ingredients at home. Natural and homemade products are safe for skins that are prone to allergy because we know what ingredients are included in the product and that they are all natural. While the products that are made conventionally can contain a certain chemical that might be harmful to your skin and you wouldn't know that. So to play safe, it is good for people who are allergic to a lot of different stuff to use natural and homemade products.

4. Homemade natural products are safe for your nose and head.

Conventionally manufactured products contain certain artificial odors to give them a pleasant appeal. These odors contain lots of different chemicals that can be harmful to your nose. These odors are added to cover up the pungent and bad smell of different chemical used in these products. These odors can cause a serious headache and if you keep using such products, you would get a permanent headache problem. Natural and homemade products don't use any harmful chemicals to give them a special scent. Instead, they use the natural scent of the organic and natural ingredients added to make them. Natural products are usually scented with natural essential oils that are not only sweet smelling but they are also very good for your nose and for your brain, so much so that they provide aromatherapy.

5. **Natural products that are made at home have no strange side-effects.**

Products that are conventionally manufactured in industries and large scale factories use Parabens in them. Parabens are added to increase the lifetime of the products and to make them last for long. Parabens, are synthetic preservatives that are added to mimic the natural hormones of your body. These preservatives can change how your endocrine system should work. Parabens can help do one function well but there are many other side-effects of this preservative. Side-effects that cannot be reversed sometimes. The side-effects are usually hidden and are only known when the effect has gone too far. Whereas natural homemade products are made from pure natural ingredients such as essential oils, grapefruits extracts, extracts of different seeds etc. Many people may be allergic to some of these natural products, like lanolin which comes from wool and it causes allergy to some people. But the side-effects and allergy caused by natural elements can be understood much more easily than those caused by synthetic and artificial products.

6. **Natural products become gentler with time.**

Products that are made commercially in large factories can work for you in the beginning but in the long run, you would start to understand that they are causing bad effect on your skin too. Whereas the natural products made from natural and organic materials may work slowly but they will keep working for you. They are not as fast as synthetic products but they are better. How? They get gentler with time. When you keep using natural homemade products, you would realize that with time, your skin is getting used to the natural product and it is not only doing what it is supposed to do but it is also helping you in many ways. Like many products can not only help you keep away from insects but they will also keep your skin nice and soft.

The above mentioned benefits may seem small but they are, in the long run, really beneficial. You should compare take a good look at these benefits and decide for yourself if you want to keep using the synthetic products with harmful chemicals or you want to change your routine and find the better alternative of these harmful products which is the natural and homemade products made from organic and environment/skin friendly ingredients.

Chapter 3 – 5 Recipes for Natural and Homemade Mosquito Repellents

In this chapter, I would share with you some really easy and useful recipes that you can use to protect you and your family from mosquito attacks. You have learnt in the previous chapter why you should use natural and homemade products. If you are using some artificial and synthetic mosquito repellent to repel mosquitoes, you should stop using that. You have 5 better options that are not only effective in keeping the mosquitoes away from you but they are also environment friendly, skin friendly, healthy, anti-allergic and a lot cheaper than mosquito repellents made conventionally. You can select from the following 5 recipes of very effective mosquito repellents and make one for yourself. You can make these repellents and try them first. I can assure you they will work miracles for you and they will not damage your skin in any way. These natural and homemade mosquito repellents would keep you and your family safe from mosquito attacks and would not harm your skin in any way because they contain no hidden artificial chemicals. The greatest advantage is that you would know what you are using in making these repellants and you would be sure that they contain nothing that is harmful to your skin or your health in any way.

Let's have a look at some of these useful mosquito repellent recipes.

Natural mosquito Repellent Spray:

To make this mosquito repellent spray, you would need the following ingredients,

- Boiled or distilled water (2 ounces) (cool the water down before you use it)

- Citronella oil (30 drops)

- Peppermint oil (25 drops)

- Witch hazel or Vodka (1 ½ ounces)

- Tea tree oil (15 drops)

- Vodka or witch hazel: 1.5 ounces

- Jojoba oil (1 tsp) – Add this oil with 1 ounce of vodka or witch hazel.

Directions:

Take a spray bottle that could contain 4 ounces of liquid. Fill the bottle with water. Now add vodka or witch hazel. Add 50 to 70 drops of jojoba oil or any other essential oils. Shake this well and spray this mixture on your body and your clothing. Keep this mixture away from heat or sunlight. Keep it safe in a cool place. Avoid the eye area when you spray this mixture on your body. Apply this mixture every 2 hours to keep it working. The essential oils should be therapeutic grade essential oils.

Essential Oil Blends:

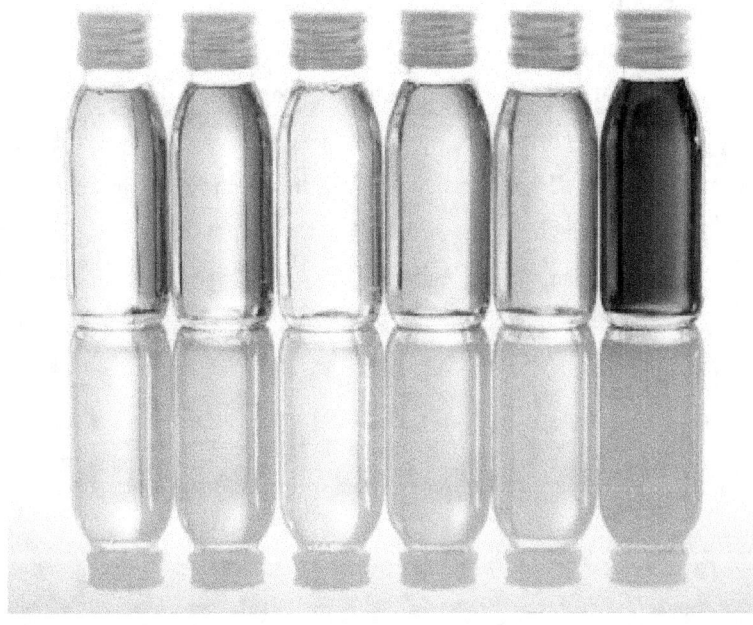

http://i2.wp.com/blackgirllonghair.com/wp-content/uploads/2012/01/essential_oils.jpg

This mosquito repellent is really effective and it is made from some really useful essential oils. To make this repellent, you would need the following ingredients,

- Cedar wood oil (10 – 12 drops)

- Rosemary oil (10 - 12 drops)

- Lavender oil (10 - 12 drops)

- Lemon Eucalyptus oil (30 - 35 drops)

- Vodka or witch hazel

Directions:

Take a small bottle and mix all the above mentioned oils in the small bottle. Add vodka or witch hazel to this mixture. Now shake the bottle well to mix all the ingredients. Apply this blend of essential oils on your skin to protect yourself from mosquitoes. Remember don't apply this repellent on the skin of children younger than 3 years. Keep it in a safe, dry and cool place. Don't put it in the sunlight.

Lavender Mosquito repellent:

http://www.purenaturalsimple.com/wp-content/uploads/2014/05/lavendar-300x200.jpg

This mosquito repellent is really effective and you should use it to keep yourself and your family safe from mosquito bites. This recipe includes the following ingredients,

- Vanilla extract (3 – 4 tbsp)

- Lavender oil (15 drops)

- Distilled or boiled water (cool the water down before you use it)

- Lemon juice (1/4 cup)

Directions: Take a small spray bottle and put all these ingredients in the bottle. Shake this mixture together in the spray bottle. Apply this mixture on your skin to repel mosquitoes. Keep it away from sunlight and heat. Safely place it in a cool and dry place away from children's reach. This spray can last for six months.

Cloves Mosquito Repellent:

This is another really useful mosquito repellent that you can make at home. This is skin friendly and very effective in keeping mosquitoes and other insects away. This repellent can be made from the following ingredients,

- Cloves (3 ½ ounces)

- Rubbing alcohol (16 ounces)

- Baby oil (3 ½ ounces) – You could also use other essential oils like lavender, chamomile, almond oil etc whatever you like

Directions: Pour rubbing alcohol in a bowl and put the cloves in it. Leave it like this for four days so that the cloves infuse in the rubbing alcohol. Just remember to stir the cloves in the rubbing alcohol in the morning and the evening every day for four days. After four days, strain the alcohol and pour it in a bottle. Mix the oil that you like in the alcohol. Mix them well by shaking the bottle every time you use this repellent. Keep away from children and keep it safe in a cool and dry place. Don't leave in the sunlight or heat.

Garlic Mosquito Repellent:

https://authoritynutrition.com/wp-content/uploads/2014/08/garlic-on-blue-wooden-board.jpg

This mosquito repellent is really effective. You would be using the benefits of garlic to protect yourself and your family from mosquito bites. To prepare this useful repellent, you would need the following ingredients,

* Few cloves of garlic (minced)

* Mineral oil

* Lemon juice (1 tsp)

* Distilled or boiled water (2 cups) (cool the water down before you use it)

Directions: Take a few cloves of garlic and mince them. Now cover the minced garlic with mineral oil. Leave this for a day to let it sit. After a day, take a teaspoon of mineral oil and mix it with 2 cups of distilled or boiled water. After that, add 1 teaspoon of freshly extracted lemon juice. Take a cheese cloth and strain this mixture. Now when the mixture is without floaties, pour the liquid into a spray bottle and spray it on your body to protect yourself from mosquito attacks. Keep away from heat and sunlight. Keep this spray safe in a cool and dry place. Shake the bottle well before you spray it on your body.

I have shared with you the recipes of these really effective mosquito repellents. You can make this at home with your own hands. These would not only keep you safe from mosquito attacks but they will also be good to your skin. These mosquito repellents would not cause any reaction to your skin like the synthetic and artificial chemical mosquito repellents that you used once.

Chapter 4 – 5 Recipes for Natural and Homemade Ant Repellents and Killers

In this chapter, I would discuss with you some really useful recipes that you can follow to make some natural and homemade ant repellents. As much as people love spring, the ant problem that comes with it causes a lot of trouble. There are ants everywhere. If you have dropped a tiny chunk of some sweet food on the floor, in less than a minute, you would see ants marching up to claim their share of your sweet food that you have accidently dropped on the floor. This happens not just on the floor, your kitchen shelves are not safe either. Sometimes if you are listening to a phone call while leaning towards the wall, an ant might come from nowhere and bite you on your neck or your arm. This can be really frustrating having these nasty little beasts moving all around your house, disturbing you. It gets even worse when these ants form a colony somewhere in your house. You would know the problem has gone almost out of hand when you see a huge colony of ants at your home. You would not only need to get rid of the colony but you would also have to keep yourself and your family safe from their bites. For that purpose, I am sharing with you 5 very useful recipes of natural and homemade and repellents that you can make to keep yourself safe from ant attacks. These natural repellents would cause no harmful reaction on your skin. They are skin friendly and they are much more effective than the synthetic products that you buy from the market. As you are the maker of these repellents, you would not have to fear if they contain any harmful chemical or product that can cause damage to your health and your skin.

Let's have a look at these recipes,

Simple Insect Repellent:

This insect repellent is multi-functional, it would not only keep ants away from you, it would also keep other insects away from you. To prepare this mixture, you would need the following ingredients,

- Boiled or distilled water (1 cup) (cool the water down before you use it)

- Vinegar (1 cup)

- Lavender oil or Tea tree oil (30 – 32

- Witch hazel or Vodka (1 tsp)

Take a small spray bottle and add all the above mentioned ingredients in it. Shake the bottle to thoroughly mix all the ingredients. You natural ant repellent spray is ready. You can spray it on your body. Make sure you shake the bottle well before every use. Keep this spray bottle in a cool and dry place. Don't keep it in direct sunlight or heat.

2. Jam Bait Ant Killer:

http://4.bp.blogspot.com/-t1iRKLrM1Ow/VYFawew2VKI/AAAAAAAAGTk/p75nP-hU8Bw/s320/IMG_4163.jpg

This is a way of killing the ants. You can make this ant killing solution from the following ingredients,

- TBC Borax or Boric Acid

- Jelly, jam, sugar, maple syrup or honey

Directions: To kill the ants at your home, you can make this ant killer by mixing jelly, jam, sugar, maple syrup or honey with boric acid or TBC Borax. Make a paste with this mixture. Now take this paste and spread it on different corners of your house. The sweetness of the jelly, jam, sugar, maple syrup or honey would attract the ants and they would eat this mixture. This is where boric acid or TBC borax would do its job. The poison would kill the ants. When the ants approach this mixture, don't get impatient and start killing them, wait and let them take this mixture back to their colony. They would share this poisonous food with their colony and this way you would be able to kill a lot more ants than you think you could. Keep this paste away from the reach of children.

Orange Peels to Kill and Repel Ants:

http://www.blessedhomestead.com/wp-content/uploads/2013/04/lemon.jpg

This is another very useful ant repellent that you can make at home with the help of orange peels. This would help you not only to repel ants but also to kill them. You will need the following things to make this ants repellent and killer,

- Blender

- Distilled or boiled Water (one cup) (cool the water down before you use it)

- Several orange peels

Directions: Take the blender and pour a cup of boiled or distilled water in it. Take the orange peels and put them in the blender too. Turn on the blender and blend the mixture well until it is smooth. You can increase the amount of this blend by increasing the number of orange peels and water and blending them together. Now you can use this blend and pour it on the hills of ants that you see around your house. This would kill the ants. You can also put this solution in a spray bottle to spray it on the areas that are affected by ants. You can also spray this mixture on the outer base of your house to keep the ants from coming into the house. This way you can not only kill the ants but you can also block them from entering your house and biting you and your family.

Protein Baits:

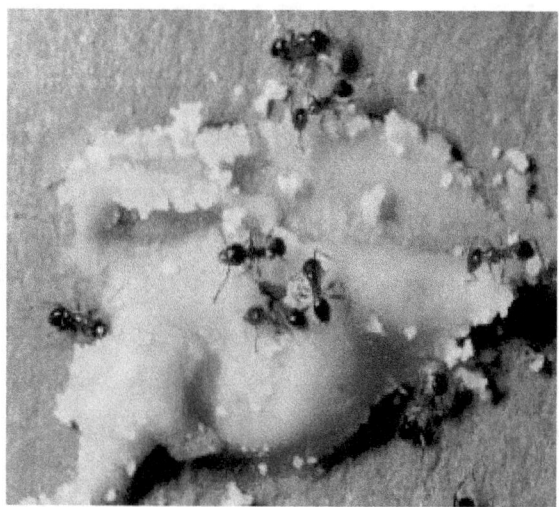

This works just like jam bait for ants. One ingredient is different. You can make this at home to keep away from ants and to kill them. You would need,

* Bacon grease or peanut butter
* Boric acid or TBC Borax (2 tbsp)

Directions: Take a bowl and add the ingredients mentioned above in the bowl. Mix both of the ingredients well to make a paste. Now put this paste on a piece of paper and put it in different places in your house. This is a bait to kill the ants. The ant would come to claim their "food" but they don't know that it's poisonous to them. Don't start killing them when they march towards the food, wait for them to take this food home to their family. This way the whole colony can be destroyed with just two ingredients. Keep this paste away from the reach of children.

Simple Natural Ant Repellents:

These simple natural things can be used to keep ants away from your home. You can find all these things in your kitchen or pantry,

- Black Pepper (powdered)

- Table salt

- Citrus

- Boiling water and dishwashing soap

- Lemon juice

- Cinnamon powder

- Vinegar

- Chalk

- Bay leaves

- Red chili powder

- Cucumber peels

- Baking soda and powdered sugar

- Cream of wheat

- Cloves

- Red pepper flakes

- Coffee (ground)

- Salt

- Sage

- Cornmeal

- Essential oils: Lavender oil, peppermint oil, eucalyptus oil etc.

You can swab these things at different points in your house. Swab these at the entrance of your house especially to keep the ants from coming into your house.

You can use the above mentioned recipes of killing ants keep your home and your family safe from ant bites. You could save your food from those sudden marches too. You can do all this with ingredients that are already found at your home. Good luck!

Conclusion

The recipes that I have given in this book are not only easy but the ingredients required for their making are also readily available. You can make these mosquito and ant killers at home with organic and natural stuff. You don't have to fear for any side effects too. If you are allergic to one of the ingredients used in one of the mosquito repellents, you can try out some other recipe.

The ants killing and repelling recipes are really easy too. You can use them to keep your family and yourself safe from ants.

These natural products are environment friendly and they are not harmful to your health too. The only health they are harmful to, is the mosquito's or ant's health which is what you really want.

Try out these simple homemade and natural recipes to make mosquito or ant repellents and killers for you and your family and you would not think about using the synthetic chemical products ever again.

FREE Bonus Reminder

If you have not grabbed it yet, please go ahead and download your special bonus report *"Leptin Resistance. 21 Leptin Recipes For Weight Loss & Healthy Living"*.

Simply Click the Button Below

OR **Go to This Page**

http://easyweightlossway.com/free/

BONUS #2: More Free & Discounted Books

Do you want to receive more Free & Discounted Books?

We have a mailing list where we send out our new Books when they go free or with a discount on Kindle. Click on the link below to sign up for Free & Discount Book Promotions.

=> Sign Up for Free & Discount Book Promotions <=

OR Go to this URL